Educa

What's So Special ~~about~~ Special Education?

Having spent many hours in classes to become a teacher of special education, I can speak from real experience when I recommend Mrs. McBrine's book as an essential compendium for special education classes. It is written with humor, compassion and real how-to suggestions for, not only the novice in special education, but also for those who are veteran teachers.

Susan McKenzie,
Teacher of preschool children with disabilities, 20 years experience

Mrs. McBrine's powerful experiences have helped her to relate to teachers and parents of our "life changers," as she describes our students. I sincerely thought her book was educational, informative and inspiring. I would truly recommend her book to parents and new teachers. As teachers, we can not completely imagine how hard it might be to raise children with special needs. Therefore, we should always make parents feel like their hard work is appreciated and acknowledged. Reading her book reminded me that I am an influence on my students and their families. It reaffirmed to me why I am an educator. At the end of the day when I go home, I can leave with the peaceful thought that I made a difference in the life of a child.

Laura Doamozy,
2nd year teacher, Special Education center based school

As a first year teacher in the SH setting, McBrine's insights on issues such as understanding parents, IEPs, and medical issues were beneficial in many ways that can not, or are not, being taught in college courses. As a teacher and a parent, she provides a needed perspective for me to improve my own skills. Chapters 2 and 5 really clear up many questions I have had. Some days, I do feel overwhelmed and reading her writings truly showed me that the supportive environment is most important and that every day has its own successes.

Monica Romero,
IVCEC special education teacher, 1st year, elementary level.

If you are a newly minted teacher of special needs students, please read this book and keep a copy in your desk. Read it in September and when you have a difficult time with a student. Read it before an IEP meeting to gain understanding of what it takes to be a parent of one of our students. Susan's experience, both as a mother of a special needs child and her expansive experience as a teacher of both general ed and special ed students, gives her the knowledge and awareness of what it takes to get up every day and make a difference in our students' lives. She has provided me much help as I have learned how to be effective in the classroom. Her words are golden coins, great gifts of awareness and love, to bring to our classrooms.

Barbara McAndrews,
teacher of special education SH on general ed campus

A practical straight-forward book written for special education teachers that addresses many relevant topics not typically found in standard teacher training texts. The writer shares first-hand experience as both a loving parent and special education teacher. This first-hand information is essential for teachers because it provides unique insight in how to successfully deal with a plethora of issues the teacher of special needs children is confronted with on a daily/weekly/yearly basis .

Dr John Caltigirone,
Administrator, principal, Imperial valley center for exceptional children

Since its inception, the Tuberous Sclerosis Alliance has been committed to providing fellowship, generating awareness, pursuing knowledge and providing hope to those who shared the common bond of tuberous sclerosis complex. These goals remain the driving force of the organization today. We are proud of one of our founding moms, Susan McBrine, for her important effort to provide valuable information in this book for educators about the needs of children with severe disabilities and how to communicate with their parents. Forty years after Susan founded the TSalliance, we remain an organization committed to the rallying the resources, the research, the partnerships and the sheer will of TSC-affected families and individuals, to break the back of this linchpin disease, which is the leading cause of epilepsy and autism.

Kari Luther Rosbeck,
CEO and president , Tuberous Sclerosis Alliance

This book gives special education teachers clear guidance and support for effective teamwork with families of children with different abilities.

Dr Kim Huynen,
behavioral psychologist and, founder/administrator of Del Sol School

WHAT'S SO SPECIAL ABOUT SPECIAL EDUCATION?

PRACTICAL TIPS FOR TEACHERS TO WORK EFFECTIVELY WITH PARENTS

Susan McBrine

LUMINARE PRESS

WWW.LUMINAREPRESS.COM

What's So Special About Special Education?
Practical Tips For Teachers To Work Effectively With Parents
© 2015 Susan McBrine

Printed in the United States of America

Cover Photos used with permission of parents
Cover Design: Claire Last

Luminare Press
467 W 17th Ave
Eugene, OR 97401
www.luminarepress.com

ISBN: 978-1-937303-67-9
LCCN: 2015958027

To my children,
Stacia (now an angel), Tanya, Mitch and Kara

CONTENTS

What Is So Special about Special Education?

THIS BOOK HAS GREAT INSIGHT FOR TEACHERS IN UNDER-standing how to work with parents of children with special needs.

In reality parent engagement is the only way a child with special needs can receive an appropriate education. Many school systems say they want parent involvement but don't know how to make that happen. Teachers and administrators need to understand how to talk and work with parents of children with special needs. This book will provide insight for anyone who reads it. Anytime we can find a tool to help better outcomes for student with disabilities we need to utilize that tool. "What is So Special about Special Education?" is a useful tool to be utilized by any education professional working with student with special needs.

In my position as Vice President of Outreach for the National Tuberous Sclerosis Alliance, I work with many school systems through out the country in understanding tuberous sclerosis complex. Tuberous sclerosis complex (TSC) is a genetic disorder that causes non-malignant tumors to form in many different organs, primarily in the brain, eyes, heart, kidney, skin and lungs. The aspects of TSC that most strongly impact education are generally associated with the brain: seizures, developmental delay, intellectual disability, autism, and many types of learning disabilities. Because TSC is rare and can change quickly, depending on the individual's manifestations, it is vital that school systems work closely with parents. In my experience many regular, and even special education teachers, do not know how to work with or even talk to parents of children with special needs.

—Dena Hook, Vice President of Outreach
Tuberous Sclerosis Alliance

FOREWORD

THIS PRACTICAL SOURCE BOOK WILL BENEFIT BOTH BEGINning and experienced teachers working in this specialized field of moderate/severe disabilities. This book offers sound advice for an array of significant cognitive and physical disabilities. As a parent of a daughter with tuberous sclerosis who is severely affected, Mrs McBrine offers a unique perspective of both parent and teacher. The book bridges the gap that often exists between the home environment and the school setting. It provides a needed input on how to foster positive teacher/parent relationships, especially during a time of increased fair hearings and litigation.

The book offers succinctly written chapters addressing teacher priorities, IEPS and parent conferences, medical issues in the classroom, transition to adult services and the future of special education. The book not only provides information on what to teach, but also provides some teaching methods and materials. The user friendly book will be an invaluable addition to the professional library of all teachers who desire to navigate triumphantly through, what can sometimes be, the very challenging terrain of special education. Written from a real life look into the dynamics surrounding home and school, the book's aim is for the teachers to be equipped with what they need to know in order to develop a cohesive relationship with parents and professionals, which will result in maximizing students' special education programs and preparing them for the best possible future — a shared goal. John Caltagirone, Ed.

—Dr. John Caltagirone
Principal, Imperial Valley Center for Special Education and
Imperial County Office of Ed Special Ed Programs (retired)

CHAPTER ONE

WHY READ THIS BOOK?

I AM WRITING THIS BOOK TO GIVE TEACHERS, ESPECIALLY those new to special education, an understanding of what I like to call the "world of those with disabilities or special education." It is an understanding most people would not otherwise come to for a long time, if ever, unless they relate to the children through their families and what they want and need for their children. Primarily I am directing this book at those who work with whom special education, in California at least, calls SH or Severely Handicapped. Much of this book could apply, however, to all special education populations.

It is the SH population and its teachers working on the moderate to severe disabilities certification, who seem to be neglected somewhat in special education training. Teaching students with severe disabilities requires a much less book oriented or academic methodology. It is vastly more challenging to come up with appropriate curriculum and training for teachers since the students' needs are so unique and their learning styles so diverse due to their disabilities. It is for this very reason that special education has strived to come up with a SH-specific curriculum and appropriate manipulative materials with which to teach, where once there were little to none available. Things are improving, however, as more and more former teachers of SH students are becoming involved in designing curriculum, materials, and training. There are now more catalogs available to order student- specific, disability-specific materials for limited or non-readers, which are age appropriate, and/or materials to address behaviors or sensory issues

Most SH teachers can tell you that workshops, classes, and conferences are few and far between which really pertain to many of the types of challenges and teaching situations they face in every classroom. However, I think it is profoundly important for teachers and administrators to realize that teachers of SH students will find their jobs so much more successful and enjoyable if they understand how to communicate and empathize with the parents first. Most other teachers will never work as closely with parents, as will the teachers of those children who may not speak or be able to learn in traditional ways or with traditional curriculums, due to the severity of their disabilities.

SH teachers wear many hats during the day. They are, at times, social workers, nurses, counselors, artists, computer specialists, data keepers, and supervisors of instructional aides, in addition to being instructors. So much more multitasking goes on in a SH classroom, because teachers are not using textbooks or teacher's guidebooks as much as general ed teachers do. They teach from IEP goals, games, manipulatives, behavior plans and creative lesson plans designed to individually teach a child who may not have been sitting up or speaking the year before.

In any one class, a teacher may have a child who is a reader, a non-reader, a child who is also physically disabled, a child with a behavior or seizure disorder, an autistic child, and more. Every classroom and lesson plan has to be individualized to teach the child and how he/she is affected by his/her disability. SH teachers must communicate with the parents to understand how to reach and teach the child. It is often difficult for an in experienced teacher to talk to parents, but it is something he or she needs to master and not to fear.

I am the parent of four, now adult, children. The eldest, Stacia, was born with a neuro-degenerative disorder called tuberous sclerosis complex, diagnosed at 9 months old. Her diagnosis eventually included developmental disability (severe), dual diagnosis of autism, behavior disorders, seizures, and the related medical problems associated with some TSC cases – brain, eye and kidney tumors, sleep and appetite problems, later a feeding tube and eventually kidney failure. I raised her at home for 27 years and then placed her in a group home the last three years of her life before she died in 2003. She was in special education in California from the age of 18 months to age 22. She attended classes on a center based campus and on a general Ed high school campus.

I was also a teacher with two teaching credentials, one in secondary English and one in special education with a specialty in severe to moderate disabilities. I became a teacher in 1970 of high school and junior high English and journalism, switching to Special education in 1989 when I finally realized I could teach kids with disabilities all day and still go home to Stacia with all of her problems and my other three kids without going bananas! It was a change I never regretted. I taught learning disabled first and then changed after two years to SH, the level where Stacia was functioning and the level where I felt I could make the biggest difference. I taught SH for the next 16 years on all age levels, spending most of the years with the high school age group of 16-22 years old. I am now retired from teaching after 37 years. As you can see, I have some practical experience on both sides of the IEP table, as a parent and as an educator. These teaching experiences were enriching and life changing, as were those of being a parent. I knew how it felt to prepare a classroom and to write an IEP, as well as how it felt to be a parent discussing my own child at her IEP. I also saw special education go through great changes and evolve from the 1970s to the present. These changes were for the better and gave parents more involvement in their child's IEP and education.

During my years raising children, I learned a great deal from my three children, now adults, Tanya, Mitch, and Kara. I learned the most, however, from Stacia about how to be an effective teacher and about special education. I learned if you can teach a child with severe disabilities a simple task, you can also learn to teach other more complex ideas and processes. She changed my life, my professional goals and my perspective on everything I have known or hope to know. I really believe that those people who have never been exposed to the world of special education (or developmental disabilities or mental retardation) are missing something in life. They haven't had the opportunity to see life through the eyes of children and adults who don't know how to complicate matters or not be themselves.

The term for these children or label isn't important to me as a parent or as a professional. Getting hung up on the latest politically correct term doesn't change the child or the parent, as long as no one lets that label change how our children are treated. Only other people can make terms like mental retardation, trainable, special or slow be negative words. Parents and teachers of these children know they are people first and have value and purpose in life, no matter what they are called. Of course none of us want out children to be labeled or disrespected

In the UK, as well as here, they also often call these children, children with "Special needs." Maybe that is the best term. For surely they are children first, and they have special needs. The medical profession often still uses the term, 'mental retardation' to describe our children. The education profession has changed terms over the years, presently settling on 'Developmentally disabled" or cognitively impaired. Whatever year and whatever term is used, I think perhaps these children should be called "life changers," because if you are around them long enough they will change your life and the way you view the world.

During my teaching career, I often mentored and helped new teachers in this field. Partly as a result of the shortage of teachers in special education, I found that many were thrown in to the classroom with little or no experience, working hands-on with any student with special needs. Many were working on their credential AFTER they were hired with just a Bachelor's degree, sometimes from a completely unrelated field. Some finished their credential course work first, but had no student teaching or even experience with kids at all. Lastly, some thought they knew what they were getting into, but really had no idea whether they would like the field or the kids. When I talked to them after the first month, they were often overwhelmed, exhausted and wondering whether they made any difference or would even survive their first year. I heard things from them they couldn't or wouldn't tell an administrator and most of it was frustration with how difficult the job was and how much was expected. So many felt their training left out a great deal of reality. Usually, as the year went by the frustrations eased and they came to love the kids, although the job may not have become less difficult.

The course requirements seem to have become increasingly more difficult and the costs more expensive to become a teacher. Unfortunately, with the increased requirements has not always come increased compensation. It is one of the few professions which requires one to three years of graduate school, yet the starting pay is not comparable with other professions which require this much education. Most of us go into the field for the love of children, not salary. I hope this book will help new teachers to survive, to really know how to understand these children and their families and to love the profession they have chosen.

Susan McBrine

Chapter Two

Understanding Parents

WHAT DO PARENTS AND THEIR CHILD GO THROUGH BEFORE that child reaches your classroom?

Most new teachers have no idea how much energy, patience, and determination it takes for a parent to just get that child on the bus or car to school, sometimes after a sleepless night for both parent and child. The medical, physical, behavioral and cognitive challenges which the family faces every day and many nights are often huge. All the special ed courses in the world do not prepare a teacher for the first time he/she sees a student have a seizure, a behavior outburst or an inability to sit still in a desk to concentrate for even minutes. One asks, "How do I teach, when the child can't or won't pay attention and has so many physical and developmental problems?" Yes, you learned about these in a book, but the book never prepares you for the reality of a child looking to you for a way to help him learn.

To teach, you have to also understand some things about the family and the birth of this child. Then you have to understand each child is a child first, a person first, then a person with a disability. Once you are able to do this, you'll stop thinking about yourself as a special education teacher. You'll be a teacher who just happens to teach students, who just happen to be a bit different from the ordinary. And different isn't good or bad—just different. By the end of the year, you'll be talking about your students and class as any teacher would, not just about their disabilities. All of your friends and family will probably tire of hearing you talk about " your kids " and how proud you are of Janie or Jose who learned to count to 10 or finally stopped banging on his desk. They may wonder why in the world you do this every day, but you won't!

As the year goes by and you slowly learn how to reach these kids, how to organize your class, write Individual Education Plan goals, train your aides etc., you finally begin to feel successful. Classroom management is being mastered. Then, you go into the teachers' room and you hear others complaining about parents. Sounds something like...*If only the mom would cooperate* or *If only the parents were consistent, Jimmy or Susie would respond.* Sometimes even more unflattering words are used like, *Those parents are just plain weirdos* and *Don't they care about that kid? Why don't they return my call? Why do they send her to school sick? Didn't they check his backpack?.* . . and more. I've heard it all and sometimes I've said it myself.

All parents are different and all parents have different parenting skills and styles. Nowhere do these differences and abilities (or lack of), affect a child and a classroom more than in special education, however. The more you know about how to deal with parents effectively and understand where they are coming from, the easier your job will be. Countless new teachers have complained to me they don't know how to talk to or get the parents on their side or to help with their goals for the child in their class. It is not always learned in a college class.

I once had my daughter's special ed teacher tell me (during my first year as a SH teacher) that the hardest part of teaching was working with the parents. I didn't understand what she meant at first. Then she said "I love the kids, but the parents make my job so hard." I think she forgot for a minute that I was one of "those" parents of a child in her class. I never forgot that comment and it is one of the reasons for this book. I thought to myself, *Believe me, working with my Stacia was a lot harder than working with me; after all I was potty trained.* Yet, working with the parents can be more difficult if a teacher does not have the understanding of the parent's life while raising a child with a disability.

My daughter was one who was often described as "challenging, difficult, and really special" because her disability involved neurological behaviors and seizures and medication side effects. Her abilities and behaviors were up and down on a day-to-day basis. Sometimes she would lose ground due to a new medication or an operation. Sometimes she would have new and unusual behaviors due to seizure activity or a new medication we tried to control the seizures. A lot of what she did and didn't do was beyond her control or ours. I am sure she was often the topic of conversation in the teacher's room and the biggest pain in a classroom, even though she, thankfully, had many funny and lovable moments and genuinely liked school and people. I knew, realistically, sometimes her teachers were glad when she was absent, just as I was glad she was at school! Once she told her teacher she got her orthodontic braces at Kmart's blue light special—we still don't know where she got that idea. At least she gave them some good laughs.

Parent and teachers have to be brutally honest about these children. We parents have to love them, support them and expect, hopefully, they will learn to the best of their ability. We as teachers have to expect them to learn and keep expecting them to learn, no matter how slowly or how differently, and to treat them with respect and care equally. Loving or liking them may come later, but at least teachers can send them home at 3 p.m. everyday – parents don't have that option. Teachers give their students their best, but they, like parents, have to admit that it is downright hard to work with some students. Parents also have to admit that it is often difficult to work with their own children. No one said parenting would be easy and no one said teaching would be easy. They have so much in common!

So before a teacher tries to understand the child and communicate with the parent, as we must do in special education so many times daily and weekly, —a teacher has to first understand and place him or her self in the shoes of the parent. That is easier to do if the teacher is a parent himself, but believe me the usual parenting experience is different! Becoming a parent of a child with serious disabilities is like becoming a race car driver without ever having been in a car… You don't know where the gears are or how fast to drive or even where to turn… And sometimes you need to know where the brakes are in a hurry.

Let's start with birth – For those of you who are parents, you may remember how happy the pregnancy was: planning, thinking of a name, dreaming about the college your child would attend; the prom she'd dress up for, the football games he'd star in… All the joyous experiences and love you'd share once that child came home with you. If you're not a parent, think about becoming one and how you'd feel. These parents may later be told their child is "slow for his age" or "he'll outgrow it "or they may receive a devastating diagnosis at birth or even in utero. Neighbors and even relatives will want to congratulate them on the birth, but won't know what to say, whether to express joy or sorrow, so they say nothing or offer unsolicited advice. Sometimes the friends and family just stop coming around. Every set of parents can remember clearly the words the doctor said when diagnosing their child with a disability …the moment time stood still and they found out that all the dreams and hopes they had for their child died. "It almost felt like the child you gave birth to died and another came to take its place", said one parent to me and I remember that's how I felt too.

Now, depending on the parents and their particular tolerance level for dealing with emotional pain, their parenting skills they learned primarily from their family, their spiritual beliefs, their mental health, their education level and intelligence and many other factors which we can't even begin to understand—they go into one of the stages of experiencing grief. Denial, anger, guilt, sadness, acceptance. For many parents the last stage, acceptance, is the hardest to come to, yet it is the most important. Until parents can accept that child for who she or he is, not who they wanted him or her to be, they will find it hard to function in many ways. Especially will they find it hard to deal with the education process, where it becomes distressingly obvious their child is not achieving progress the way other children his/her age are progressing.

For me, the day I heard the diagnosis from a doctor was in the emergency room with my first child, a then 9-month-old daughter. She was, until then, a perfectly normal-looking, and developing baby, who had begun to have a series of unexplained "infantile spasms." No doctor had seen these or even believed me for weeks. Finally, I took her to the emergency room after 9 different episodes in one day. So far I had been told I "was an overprotective first time mom, imagining things" etc. That day, that doctor took one look at her and told me she had "tuberous sclerosis, would be mentally retarded and probably not walk or talk." I cried all the way home. He had one other patient, age 12, with tuberous sclerosis, the only other case he had ever seen.

Most parents do go into shock, denial, then perhaps anger, guilt, sadness and someday, hopefully, acceptance and hope. They all have different timetables for these stages and some go back and forth in the stages. I remember being very angry at God, not guilty, just mad that this had to happen to MY child and how unfair it was she had to suffer. Every parent has a different time for reaching acceptance. For some, it is months, for some years, and for some never. Yet even with acceptance, the grief never goes away completely. Sometimes marriages break up because one or both parent can't get beyond shock and denial. Sometimes a parent finds it easier to leave than to stay and deal with the reality of an imperfect child. Divorce is very common among parents of children with disabilities. I have had friends say to me "I don't know how you do it and I don't think I could," referring to raising a child who had seizures, wasn't potty trained at age 6. etc. I knew, in a way, these friends were trying to be supportive, but they actually were being thankful it hadn't happened to them and wondering if they could cope if it did. I believe if you love your child you somehow find a way to raise them, but not everyone is able or capable of doing that or doing it well. We cannot JUDGE the parents who can't. Parents who do manage to do it, are not heroes or martyrs either, just parents struggling to raise the child they love.

Grief hits parents at different stages of their child's life when they realize that he/she isn't going to speak or walk, or reaches these milestones years after their peers do. It may hit a parent again when the teen years arrive and they realize their child won't play football, go to college or get married. It hurts all over again. The grief is always there, but acceptance means a parent moves on to help his child become the best he can be, not what a parent hoped he would be.

Parents have to help that child have as many normal experiences as other kids do—dances, sports, friends, jobs and a lot of these experiences have to be created by the parents. These experiences don't come naturally as they do to other children in other families. Teachers also have to help provide some of these regular childhood experiences—plays, dances, participating in a regular Ed class or activity, finding a job etc-

It took me a year to reach acceptance of who my daughter Stacia was and probably longer to really understand her limitations, since her diagnosis in 1972 was very rare. I remember thinking that if she was two years behind developmentally at age 4, she d only be two years behind at age 14 – I didn't realize at first that IQ doesn't change all that much and she wouldn't "catch up" but she would make some progress. The older she got the more her ability level was the same and we had to teach to her strengths and accept her weaknesses. Her weaknesses were many! Limitations can also depend on medical issues.

Some parents are still watching their dreams for their child die and are so immersed in their grief they don't know how to help their child reach his next stage, no matter how delayed that stage may be. For some parents they understand fully their child's limitations and disability. They may have researched the diagnosis or syndrome and know more than the doctor or you what their child's future entails. They want to do whatever it takes to help their child reach their potential. Most moms and dads would gladly cut off their arm or travel to the outer reaches of the world if it would cure their child. When they realize they can't be cured, they start to react in one of two ways in the school environment: supportively or critically (and sometimes even apathetically if their own inability to cope interferes.) Sometimes their criticism is justified, if the school does not, or cannot, meet their child's needs.

The parent may have a Ph.D or a grade school education. He or she may be helpful and supportive of your efforts in the classroom or that parent may be critical and demanding of your efforts, hoping that if they ask for more they will see improvement in their child. Yet sometimes they need to advocate for services. That parent may always be angry at the system, because he is still angry that fate gave him a child less than perfect. Usually by the time a child reaches the teen years, the parent has come to terms with their child's limitations and knows what he can expect his child to get out of his education and at what level he will achieve. Both parents and educators must tread a fine line of having high expectations and hope for progress to be made and or being unrealistic about the level of progress that CAN be achieved. Every child is different even with the same diagnosis, so it is a year by year assessment for a long time of a child's true capabilities. Sometimes the child will surprise everyone and progress beyond expectations.

Teachers will experience all types of parents and all types of children. If a teacher can understand WHY the parent is saying and doing what he is or isn't, they can begin to NOT take it personally and to even help the child and parent. If they can't help, at least they can realize the parent has yet to reach the acceptance stage. Sometimes it just helps to have the parents think about the adult years and what their dreams are for that child. Sometimes reality sets in then. Remember there is no instruction book that comes home from the hospital with this child—no developmental timetable when he will walk or talk—he sets his own. There is little counseling available and very little at no cost. Many family therapists do not understand or have little training with what a family goes thru with the sleepless nights, frequent hospitalizations, abnormal behavior and delayed development. Counseling can help immensely, as well as support groups, if either is available. Being parents of normally developing children is hard enough. Multiply the difficulty 100 times for parents of a child with a disability. It is hard on the parents, on the marriage and on the siblings. It can also turn out to be a wonderful, joyous experience, in many ways, but most families don't feel that joy for some time. They will not realize, at first, what their child's disability has to teach them about life and its ups and downs. However much they love their imperfect child, it is still very hard work raising them; much harder than raising a non-disabled child in so many ways. Finding balance in their lives and getting help and respite from the strain of 24-hour care is needed. Financial strains due to increased medical costs and child care costs are another factor. Trying to maintain a normal family life for their other children and their marriage relationship, when their life may be one medical or behavior crisis after another, is extremely difficult.

Once teachers start to understand the child's abilities in their class, then they need to try to make a point to learn about his particular disability. One needs to know what medication the child takes and why, what causes the disorder and what are the characteristics/symptoms of the disorder. This is so important so a teacher knows what a child is able to control and what he is incapable of controlling. Gaining this knowledge should start with the parent and also the support group for that particular syndrome/disorder (autism society, tuberous sclerosis alliance, down syndrome association, etc.) The internet is a godsend. Most of the syndrome-specific support groups have the latest and best information for teachers and parents. The parent may or may not know about a support group. The psychologist, social caseworker and nurse may be a knowledgeable resource and or they also may be unaware of support groups. The more teachers know, the more teachers can help the child, support personnel, and the family.

In my daughter's case, very few, even in the medical profession, were then knowledgeable about her disorder, so I, as a parent, found myself educating them. Out of sheer desperation, in 1974, I co-founded what is now the Tuberous Sclerosis Alliance, a support and research organization. What is sometimes difficult for parents and professionals is when the syndrome is so rare there are no other cases in the area, then no one knows what to expect. Even with the same diagnosis, however, two different children may exhibit different characteristics or abilities. There is also an organization called NORD, National Organization for Rare Disorders, which can be accessed for information about support groups and specific information. Most organizations will send you free information and brochures, etc., to share with parents and support personnel. Understanding what the child and parent are up against medically and psychologically will help you, as a teacher, and your expectations in the classroom. Teachers will still have to treat this child as a child first, who can learn despite his disability. Knowing more about his disability will help teachers find ways to reach him and access resources for help teaching him. Being a Special Ed teacher is a lot like being a mother or father of any child. Multi tasking is required and you will never have all the answers!

It helps a lot to understand WHY the parent doesn't look in the backpack every night or return your phone call right away. If you know his child doesn't sleep well at night and spends part of everyday screaming or seizing. and the parent has other children and a job… you may now realize why! At least when you send him home every afternoon, you can sleep and forget about his needs for a time while you relax and watch TV or have a meal. It is a 24-hour job for his parents and his parents don't always get the same breaks other parents get. At 17, their child may still need supervising every minute, as you would a toddler. Look at a two-year-old and think how much energy that would take over a lifetime to parent a child who may never outgrow that age and ability.

Chapter Three

The Two Most Important Things To Teach

Once teachers are aware of the medical, social, physi-cal, neurological and behavioral issues parents are facing every day, they can give the parents some questionnaires or interview forms to help the classroom teacher understand what the child likes, dislikes and what the parent sees as his strengths and weaknesses. Finding out what the child does at home is often a mind blower for the teacher, just as it is for a parent to find out what the child can and does do at school. Most schools have good pre-made forms or parent interview questionnaires to use. (See appendix for sample forms) The job of a special educator is to teach independence and appropriate behavior in public. These two things are of the utmost importance, in my opinion as a parent and as an educator. While we are entrusted to teach many other things and to address the agreed upon IEP goals and state standards, these are still the two most important things and everything else taught is related to them. I think once a teacher understands this it will help him set priorities, survive, and feel suc-cessful in the classroom.

Let me tell you why. If your own adult children have learned independence, they can support themselves, feed themselves, do their own laundry and hopefully balance their checkbook (even if it is the money you gave them.) If they can behave appropriately in public (social behavior) they will have meaningful and successful relationships which will keep them gainfully employed, happy and emotionally sound, with an extensive social network (perhaps including a spouse) of friends. Isn't that what we want for all our children?? For them to be self supporting, happy and loved? Children in special education don't learn independence and social skills naturally; they have to be taught. Teachers may be thinking, *I thought I was a teacher. I'm supposed to be teaching letters, numbers, not how to make friends and behave in a restaurant.*

You are teaching academic skills, however, when you teach independence and appropriate behavior. Teaching how to read a menu, how to order, count out money, take turns, and say "please and thank you" are all goals a teacher can relate to a state standard. Teachers need to remember, however, that what you are really teaching is independence and appropriate behavior so that this child, with all of his disabilities, can have a more independent and happy life as an adult. If your student learns independence, he will be able, at whatever level he is functioning, to take care of his own personal needs—from toileting to shaving and eventually to work for pay. If your student is taught appropriate social behavior, your student will be able to interact with others and to sit still long enough to learn. Then his family can take him to social/family activities without sacrificing a normal family life because of his disability. Someday, as an adult, he will be able to mingle in public during recreation or employment situations without being stared at or having to always have assistance. He will have learned life skills. There will be many times with many students over the years when you may feel you didn't teach enough or all your student could learn were simple tasks over and over again. You may go home at night and tell yourself that you did teach independence and appropriate behavior that day, that month, that year. That is an important accomplishment. The parents will be grateful because so many children learn better from someone other than their parents. If their child can do for himself and has some friends and is happy, the parents can breathe a sigh of relief and finally think *Wow, he will have a life in which he can be happy.*

Of course we'd like all our students to read, do math, understand concepts, but honestly some will not master all these skills. Some will, at some level, and some won't. A teacher may have a class as I did, where some could read and some could only point to a picture. Some could write their name, address and phone number and some could only trace their name. Yet they still managed to progress in independence and appropriate social skills so that when they left the class (and if they someday live on their own) they can live a happy productive life. A teacher may have 15 IEP goals he is working on with a student, but he can always, always relate them back to these two things—independence and appropriate behavior. Perhaps keeping this in mind will help you and the parent focus on the goals which are really important and realistic. Not every administrator or college professor will tell you this. They may dwell on standards and on academics, which have their importance also. But if you ask yourself at the end of the day "Did I teach independence and social skills today?" and your answer is yes, you can consider that day a success even if Johnny never did accomplish reading a sentence or knowing his colors in your class that year, despite your best efforts. I always remember that my daughter did not know her numbers or colors consistently, but she did know how to clean a table at work, fasten her seatbelt in the car, and eat in a group setting appropriately and she had friends! I have her teachers to thank for that too.

CHAPTER FOUR

THE IEP AND PARENT CON-.
FERENCES

I OFTEN THOUGHT WHILE RAISING STACIA, THAT I COULD never be a special ed teacher and sit on the other side of the IEP table as a teacher. My early experiences with IEPs in the '70s, before the Education for All Handicapped Children Act of 1975 was passed, were of parents on one side of the IEP table and a team of people on the other side seemingly trying to intimidate a parent with their knowledge. It definitely wasn't teamwork. My daughter began public school in 1975 in a TMR (trainable mentally retarded, a term no longer used) center school where there was no speech therapist, very little parent input and large class sizes. I have a friend whose daughter (now in her 50s) didn't start school until she was 12 because there were NO public school programs available. Thankfully things have changed for the better, even though I have heard many teachers say parents now have too much power and call all the shots. Maybe they do, but it is much better than having *no* special education program where kids sit at home, or parents being *told*, not *asked*, how their child's IEP should look. A partnership is so much better for all concerned. I cannot think of any parent who does not and would not want the very best for their child and to be a part of the process to help that child learn. If teachers can see the parents as part of a team and the parents can see the teachers as partners, then the whole IEP process is less intimidating for both. Let me tell you how a parent feels at an IEP. I know teachers have lots of training in how to write IEPs and even what to say to parents at IEPs, but I doubt anyone has ever told you how a parent FEELS at an IEP. First of all, the parents may or may not be educated (or even speak English) but even if they are college educated, doesn't mean they will understand all the education jargon of the IEP (ttp, ssi, iq. Capa, transition plan, etc.) Also, this is *their* child you are discussing… and for so many parents going to an IEP or parent conference means talking not only about their child's strengths and weaknesses, but it also is a reflection on their ability as a parent. For special ed parents, they know the IEP meeting is a place where they will be reminded of what their child *cannot* do, no matter how positively it is discussed. It is still a yearly reminder of how their child is *not* like other children his age, is still developmentally disabled and will probably never function at age level.

Some parents go into an IEP afraid or anxious, simply because their own experience in school was a bad one. Many go home and grieve all over again. Parents of children in special ed don't always get to brag about their child's homerun or his report card to the family or neighbors. In fact, these parents probably don't even talk about their child's progress or lack of progress to others anymore. It is too painful for them and most friends and family don't want to hear it because they feel guilty their child is normal or they feel pity for you and yours. Even though the parent may feel like standing on a mountaintop and shouting for joy when their child is finally potty trained at age 8, no one else really wants to hear it. None of these feelings make you feel good as a parent and so many parents stop talking about their child to anyone outside of the therapy room or classroom or to other parents of special ed children. I ended up, after years of raising Stacia, having only friends who also worked in special education. No one else really understood what my life was like. The IEP meeting, the school, is the one place where they can talk about their child and hopefully, if the school has done its job right, it is the one place where they can hear something positive about their child. Always tell the parent how much you enjoy working with their child. Find something, anything, to smile and brag about to the parents. They need to know that their child is cared for and is thought of in positive terms. The parents need that because the IEP, in itself, is a reminder their child is not like other children. By the time their child is 18 or 21, most of them have heard it all, but it still hurts to hear that Johnny is functioning on a 4 year old level and has finally learned to put his backpack away and count to 10. Although this may be cause for rejoicing, it is still sad for parents to hear when they are aware that others his age are doing algebra and reading the books in their back packs.

Let the parent talk at the IEP! I have been at IEPs that were programmed to get the parent in and out in 15 minutes. No one talked or listened and a lot was left unsaid that could've helped the child and the IEP team. I even had one administrator fall asleep during an IEP. Parents need to feel safe here. You can still get down to how to successfully handle a serious behavior problem or learning difficulty, but it is important to make them feel they are helping and know they are part of the team's decisions. Sometimes you will find they need your help to know how to follow through at home. Sometimes the IEP team will learn something about the home or medical situation that affects the IEP goals themselves from the parents' sharing. After all, the parents know their child better than anyone at the meeting. Know what resources are available in your district and community for services. The IEP team cannot do everything for a parent, but they can refer them to resources that can help the parent if the school is unable to provide or fund a resource. I think every teacher needs to be familiar with the social services available for referral. The parent will look to this team for help raising their child. Despite common assumptions, all doctors and case workers aren't always seen as available, and often do not take time discuss the concerns many parents have. Many times it is the teacher or school they come to for assistance first, and referring them to a resource outside the school may help the parent deal with issues and concerns affecting their child.

The difficult, demanding parent, as I have heard them described, may only be difficult, remember, because he is stuck in denial or anger or is overwhelmed. Sometimes that anger is directed at the school, teacher or class room in an effort to make things better or hope that by demanding more (more IEP goals, more services, etc.) will somehow cure their child or help them come to acceptance. Every parent wants whatever will help their child the most to be available. One can't blame parents for that, but if their wants are unreasonable, unrealistic or the language becomes angry or abusive at an IEP, try to remember not to take it personally. A teacher has to do the job the best they can. You may not agree with or change parents' minds, but you will be able to sleep at night, and still like and teach their child the next day, if you try to understand why the parents are difficult or demanding. Hopefully, by the end of the year, or even the end of the IEP meeting, the parent will become more supportive and collaborative. Parents sometimes need to learn that working together in a supportive manner will help their child MORE than becoming adversarial.

Also, the entire school staff needs to *always* value that parent as an *equal* partner in helping the child achieve in the classroom. It will help immensely to invite regional center caseworkers to IEPS (or social worker in your city, county.) It also helps the IEP process to talk with the parent or at least have the parents (and student if appropriate) fill out an IEP input form/questionnaire before the IEP. This talk or form should include what they feel their child is interested or needs to learn this year. This way they feel included and consulted and comfortable before they walk in to the IEP room. I would send home the form before I talked to them so they could think about what their child needed to learn before I interviewed them. Often the parents are unsure what their child's goals should be and merely agree with your recommendations or suggestions. After all, the teacher is the education expert. However, parents know what is important to *their* family. You may find, after talking to the parent, that Johnny learning to use a fork and knife at a restaurant is really important so they can take him out. Or you may learn that Jamey hugs everyone she meets and they need help teaching her not to hug strangers so they can take her out and not be embarrassed. These skills can be written into IEP goals. Again, what you are teaching involves independence and behavior. Even for those students who are more academically oriented, learning how to read a want ad and fill out a job application is teaching independence. Role playing how to behave at a job interview or ordering a meal at a restaurant is teaching appropriate social behavior.

IEP meetings will get easier and writing goals will make more sense as time goes by for a new teacher, but the *team must* be collaborative and no one should EVER dread walking into that IEP room—not the teacher to see the parent or the parent to see the teacher. If any professional in the room doesn't understand how to make a parent feel comfortable, and there may be those who don't, a teacher may find himself modeling behavior for that other professional by treating the parent the way he would want to be treated if it was his child being discussed! More and more, the students themselves are also involved in choosing/directing their IEP goals when capable and appropriate, as they should be.

CHAPTER FIVE

MEDICAL ISSUES IN THE CLASSROOM

IN THE SH WORLD, THERE ARE MANY MEDICAL AND NEUrological issues to be addressed which can affect the classroom. Not every teacher has to face a classroom full of students with chronic diseases and genetic syndromes which affect how a child performs in a class everyday, but the SH teacher does. It is a challenge to say the least. Sometimes the parent of one child will forget that teacher has to worry about the welfare and safety of every student, not just the one who has a certain disease or syndrome. Every child will have problems. Teachers are not nurses, doctors or therapists, but a teacher has to be aware of how the medical issues affects that child in order to work with that child daily. The teacher may have to consult with a doctor, nurse or therapist in order to know how to teach the child more effectively.

It is vital to know what the parent is going through at home with that child also. For example, parents may be giving daily shots, pills, special diets, therapies or using a feeding tube. Getting the morning pill dosage down before the bus comes is often an issue for the parent, especially if that bus comes at 6 or 6:30 am. Sometimes the child and parent are getting no sleep. One parent of a boy with autism told me she actually had to sleep lying down in front of the door because her son would awaken at night and go outside. Another of my students, who was almost 20 and had a syndrome that caused him to be very small for his age, was getting up every night and getting in bed with his parents. They were so worn out and didn't know how to teach him to stay in his own bed. These are tough issues for families. It helps the teacher to know about these issues.

You can't teach kids who are not awake, are so drugged up they can't function, or are having so many seizures their brain is constantly short circuiting. You will need to get the nurse or even the doctor involved with parental permission if you think the medical issues are interfering with the learning process. If you are not aware of the medical issues, however you can't try to access help or activate an IEP meeting to discuss ways to solve the problems for the child. Sometimes just a referral to the nurse or caseworker will get the child the needed medical, vision or dental help he may need. The nurse is a great ally. She talks to the parent for her triennial medical report and gives you a report. It is important to read the report. You may find out about a new medication or diagnosis the parent neglected to tell you about. Keeping those lines of communication open is important so that parents tell you about new medicines he is trying or new procedures the child is undergoing. It isn't good to find out in April that a child hasn't been taking his behavior meds for months because he won't eat in the morning and the doctor said he had to take the meds with food. This is a typical problem, easily solved by having him take the meds at school after a snack.

If your principal doesn't already provide you with a good home questionnaire (see appendix), make your own with approval. This is a valuable tool at the beginning of year. The more you know the easier it is to teach these kids. If you're not aware of medicine side effects, ask your nurse or talk to the doctor who prescribed (with parental permission.) This is vital, so you know how to deal with it at school. You need to know diagnosis, symptoms and medications. For example: if you have a child with IBS and don't know what that is, you could be in trouble on your first field trip—if you don't know what it means, *ask* (IBS is irritable bowel syndrome meaning frequent necessary trips to bathroom, sort of important to know on a field trip !!)

Yes, it can be overwhelming, but it doesn't have to be. Have notebooks for each student with all the information you collect and document in a brief note, dates and times you had problems in class regarding medication or behaviors. You are often the first to know about a child's medicine not working or being too strong. If a child is having twenty seizures a day at school and none at home, mom will never know to tell the doctor to get his medication adjusted unless you kept a record. Your nurse should have seizure tracking forms or make your own. It only takes a minute, but it will help you, the child, the parent and the doctor to treat the child. Seizures are common in SH classes and seizure meds and seizure types often change with age. (see appendix for link to seizuretracker.com)

Little things can make a big difference in a teacher's day and your student's life. Document/keep records of meds, seizures, behavior episodes, and scratches they may arrive at school with. This protects the teacher and also gives the parent a record of what is happening in your class. You may notice serious illness, allergies, reactions, etc., before a parent does. After all, they get off the bus, eat, bathe and go to sleep, sometimes within three hours after they arrive home. You may spend more time during the week with the child than the parent does. Ask your administrator for forms if not given out at beginning of year. Documentation is vital for your protection, for IEP information and for parental awareness. (see Appendix)

CHAPTER FOUR

APPRECIATION

I ONCE READ THAT THE MOST IMPORTANT EMOTIONAL NEED a person has is the need to feel appreciated. When I first read this, I thought, *No, it must be the need to be loved.* However, when you think about it, being appreciated makes you feel loved. When you tell your spouse you appreciate him mowing the lawn or he tells you he appreciates the lunch you made him, it makes you feel loved, doesn't it? When your child thanks you for your help you feel loved and appreciated in your role as a parent. When your boss commends you on a job well done you feel respected and proud. Appreciation goes a long way in life and parents and students need to be appreciated, as do teachers. In the parent child relationship all parents feel appreciated when their youngsters say "thanks" or "I love you" after the parent has done something for the child. Our special kids don't always have the ability to say "thank you" or "I love you." Their parents don't get the usual appreciation for their efforts as parents, just as the teachers don't always know if their efforts are rewarded either.

Parents of children in special ed are underappreciated—they don't get the feedback most parents get. They feel lonely, isolated and unappreciated, wondering if they are doing anything right. They are often physically and emotionally exhausted from taking care of their child's many needs, as well as the needs of their spouse and other children. Feeling tired and neglected in many ways comes with the job of being a parent of a child with a disability. This is true for both moms and dads of these kids. I'm sure there are some exceptions for parents who can afford paid or live in help, but those are few. The divorce rate is high, friends often don't know how to relate to the problems the family faces with this special child. A teacher can do so much for helping these parents by being supportive of their efforts to be good parents. Your feedback may be the only time they hear they are doing a good job. Even if the parents are really struggling with the parenting skills in your estimation, it doesn't take much to help change their perception that they are good parents and may help them to strive to do even better. Some ways you can support and appreciate parents are to send notes home praising the child's progress in some area, no matter how small (this can be a form you just fill in the blank—good news notes, see appendix) Thank the parent for following thru on sending a change of clothes, or returning forms. Find something to thank them for if only for being such a caring parent because their child is so happy. The new parents of the young ones especially need this support. Not only was there no instruction book with this child, but also they are afraid they are doing everything wrong. Chances are their pediatrician doesn't have much time to talk to them and their family may not know how. You may be it. Try saying things like, "Your child looks so cute, or handsome today, thanks for being such a good mom/dad to make sure she is clean and neat." Thank them in a group note for returning forms on time and supporting your efforts. The more you appreciate their efforts, the more they will appreciate yours. A quarterly appreciation group letter to all parents will help and also prompt the ones who haven't been so supportive to step up to the plate.

Another way to show appreciation to parents is to make a big deal of mother's day and father's day. These are parents whose kids will probably never go to the store on their own or remember on their own to say happy mother's day or happy father's day. If there is any other day of the year that those feelings of grief kick in, this is one of them. Teachers can have the kids make a present or take the older ones to the dollar store to pick out and wrap a present and make a card. Try to find a special poem or article about moms or dads so they can at least feel the joy of parenthood on this day like other parents do. These gifts and cards mean more to parents of special ed kids just because their parents never thought they'd get them. I often sent home chapter 16 from Erma Bombeck's book, *Motherhood, The Second Oldest Profession,* "Why God Made You The Mother Of A Handicapped Child." Many moms said they framed it. Anything teachers do for moms on mothers' day is appreciated. It gives these moms a chance to experience what other moms take for granted.

Fathers are probably more unappreciated than moms. Mothers, women, talk to each other more than men, fathers, do and share and commiserate with other moms. Dads tend to keep their feelings inside, especially their feelings about having a child with a disability. Most parents are very proud of this imperfect child and their love is boundless, but their emotional pain is always under the surface because they worry so much about that child's future. Some fathers tend to have more difficulty dealing with the fact that they fathered an imperfect child and take longer coming to acceptance. They may not know how to help their wife with this child so they immerse themselves in their jobs or other things or they may try to fix their child by demanding more services and taking over meetings. Fathers are often neglected by the system and sometimes even by the mother. Sometimes moms are so busy meeting the physical needs of the child with a disability they forget to let the dad help also and make him feel needed. Fathers don't talk to each other as much or about their feelings of grief. Men like to solve problems and fix things —this they can't fix, so they have to learn how to help, give and accept.

It isn't easy for any parent. Some dads are wonderful and become a real partner in raising their child, some aren't. The divorce rate is extremely high in families raising a child with a disability. These children need two parents more than most. Anything a teacher can do to encourage good parenting and involvement in their child's life is a plus. Make father's day as special as mother's day. Try to include dads in class activities and encourage them to come to IEPs. I do think that fathers of this generation are much more involved in general and that all dads are making bigger efforts to be in their child's life and partners who are supportive of their wives and the teacher's efforts. A good website is listed in the appendix for fathers of special needs children.

Sharing resources or giving handouts to parents can sometimes help them come to acceptance and to learn to be more supportive of your efforts in the classroom. It always helps parents to know they aren't alone in raising a child with a disability. Any online or live support group, or even books and magazines, such as the *Exceptional Parent*, will help them to feel less isolated. After they get over the initial shock they need to read and talk about it to cope better. In my experience, parenting a child with a disability sometimes makes a marriage stronger or weakens it rapidly, due to the tremendous strains and stresses the couple faces every day. Their social life narrows drastically with the arrival of a disabled child. Their life is full of stress and it affects all relationships. Single parents are in the majority in most special education classrooms, sadly. Teachers can help parents by appreciating their efforts and praising them for their involvement.

A little appreciation goes a long way and sometimes turns a parent, who might have been critical of a class or teacher's efforts, into your biggest fan. Teachers will be pleasantly surprised at Christmas or teacher appreciation day what some parents and students will do for you or give you that will touch your heart and make YOU feel appreciated! You may be the only person—and the school the only place—the parents have felt accepted with their child and not felt they were being judged or seen as objects of curiosity. Your classroom is a safe haven for the child and the parent. You and your classroom represent a place where someone really understands their child and the daily struggles the parent faces raising that child.

CHAPTER SEVEN

LETTING GO: TRANSITIONS

LIFE IS FULL OF TRANSITIONS AS WE PROGRESS FROM ONE stage to the next. The transitions the SH children and their families go through are so much more traumatic than the usual transitions children and parents undergo. All parents have a hard time letting go! One only has to witness the scene on the first day of kindergarten as moms and dads are crying in the parking lot and the kindergarteners are crying in the classroom. Listen to older parents talk about how hard it was to drop their college freshman off at his dorm and drive away, or how a father wanted to follow his daughter on her first date. These are all normal transitions for parents and children, but not the same ones for SH children and parents.

Our SH children have transitions too, but it is harder for the parents to face these transitions or to let go. These parents have done so much FOR their child and for so much longer because their child was unable to do for himself. They don't realize always or know how to let go and stop doing FOR them, so they can learn independence and to do for themselves. Many parents of SH children have nursed them through countless medical emergencies and hospitalizations, watched and waited years for the first steps and the first words, and protected them from strangers who made fun of them or laughed at them. It is no wonder so many of the SH parents have difficulty seeing their children as adults when they do reach adulthood because their child never went through the normal age development. How does a parent learn to treat a 21-year-old as an adult when he is still cognitively on a three year old level? It is tough and frustrating for teachers also who are urging age appropriateness and independence at every stage. Nothing is harder for the high school teacher who is trying to prepare SH adults for job skills and independent living to have a parent pick their child up from school and call her or him "BABY." Yet, for that parent, part of their child will always be that helpless baby he has had to protect and advocate for all his life.

The parents' biggest concern is protection of that child from what will hurt him. Allowing him independence magnifies those concerns. The first transition occurs when they have to bring their infant or toddler to the infant/toddler class, depending on when the diagnosis was made. Leaving their child, who is perhaps medically fragile and probably non-verbal, is agony for many moms and dads. Part of them, however, is glad for the hour or two of relief and respite from the overwhelming job of taking care of a developmentally delayed child, often with little support. They are afraid their non-verbal child or behaviorally challenged child will not be taken care of, or their medical needs will be forgotten etc. Their child is likely not potty trained and that is a concern also.

The next transition is preschool where their child is learning more social skills and how to interact and sit in a group. For some parents they never thought this was possible. Integration or mainstreaming into regular ed classes may also be part of their child's day at this point. The next transition comes when he/she goes to an elementary class either on a center based campus or a regular ed campus. If this is the first time their special child is on a campus with non disabled children, the parents may worry tremendously about how the other children will treat their child. So many teachers have been heard to say these parents are overprotective, but it is hard for them not to be, when so many of them have had to struggle just to keep their child alive in the early years! Now he will begin to learn more academics and have a longer day. Parents will begin to better understand their child's differences from their peers and their child may also need other therapies in addition to the classroom. Most parents are still hoping their child will make significant progress and improve. Many do, but some don't as fast as others do. The interaction they have with non disabled children is almost always a positive thing for all involved and should be encouraged. Parents are hopefully also transitioning to acceptance of their child's disability and realizing their child's strengths and weaknesses.

The next transition is to junior high or middle school years when a child goes through puberty. With the body changes comes the parental worry of how to handle puberty issues like menstruation, shaving, and boy/girl issues. Again the parents will need help to know their child can learn to cope with these issues with assistance. The parent may need to be encouraged to treat their child as a normal adolescent, not a baby, and to dress him or her age appropriately and to remember they will go through some of the same hormonal and behavioral stages all teens go through. It is sometimes hard for parents to realize their child likes the opposite sex and all the other things teens like. Your role as a teacher is to expect the child to act his age as much as possible and to help the parent teach age appropriate behavior.

The transition to high school and the informing of the child of his legal rights before he turns 18 is the next big transition. Once the transition plans are included in the IEP (usually at age 14) the IEP team is already having discussions with the parents and child about his future and writing IEP goals for vocational and independent living. However, the ages between 18 and 22 are often the most difficult for parents. They now know their child will always have a disability and never fulfill their dreams of him or her having a completely normal adult life. Yet, they need to know their child, in most cases, can work at some supported or independent job, depending on availability in the community. The possibility of independent living may also be an option someday. I have found this discussion to be the hardest for many parents. They already have had to create a social life for their child and after he exits from school to adult vocational programs the social life revolving around school disappears. It is now up to the parent to take him/her to dances or special Olympics or dates and they don't often get invited places as an adult. If the parent doesn't create opportunities or find programs for their adult child, they find themselves sitting at home with a bored dependent child/adult. Your job as a teacher of this age group is to encourage parents to prepare for the future with their now adult child. Encourage independence, refer them to programs for social and vocational opportunities before they exit your class.

Some parents think they will live forever and have their heads firmly buried in the sand when it comes to thinking about the future of their disabled child. Many think their other adult children will voluntarily take care of their adult disabled sibling. While this may happen, it is better for the parents to plan for their adult child's future, especially if he is difficult to care for physically or needs constant supervision. Also parents may need encouragement to really consider independent living in a group home or paid roommate situation because he or she really would like to live apart from their parents as an adult, or needs to because of the demands and level of his medical care. Planting the seed to consider other living options as the child/adult ages at IEPs is helpful—parents need time to think about the possibilities. Also after age 18, the concept of limited conservatorship needs to be discussed and explained. This is called guardianship in some states. Once a child is 18 he becomes an adult legally and for a parent to continue to make decisions regarding his medical, financial, social, sexual and living arrangements, the parent must file conservatorship papers. Otherwise the adult child must be present and sign for all his legal documents, including IEPs, social security, and medical forms. He is legally able to purchase a car, go to jail, refuse or give consent for medical procedures, get married with or without parental consent. Many parents of obviously disabled children are unaware of this and really believe it is not necessary. This legal process can be done with a lawyer who specializes in disabled law or a do-it-yourself kit is available from California Regional centers and most caseworkers. This process is different than minor guardianship, which is for minors under 18. Limited conservatorship involves a court process to take away the rights of an adult and give to another court appointed adult or adults (usually in SH Cases, the parent.) This is similar to what one would do for an aged parent who becomes senile or incapacitated and can no longer make decisions about his welfare. This limited conservatorship does not mean you cannot also involve your adult child in independent decision making where possible or include him in all decisions when possible. It does give the parent the right to make all or some of the decisions for which the child is not capable of making. Every family is different and there is no timetable for filing, but they need to be aware of the possibility and then make an informed decision.

I didn't file for conservatorship until Stacia was 23, thinking anyone could see and hear that she needed me to make decisions for her as she was functioning on about a 3-year-old cognitive level and after all, I was her mother. However, when I went to pick up her blood test results at a lab one day and was told they wouldn't give them to me because she was an adult, I realized I needed to file for conservatorship. Later when she was in a group home, it gave me the right to be notified of every medication change and behavior plan, etc. I HAD to sign and give permission for the changes and later, when she became terminally ill, I had to show the papers to prove to the doctor I could make the life and death decisions that had to be made and I would not have been allowed to do without the conservatorship. I told this story at many IEPs, because I found that some caseworkers and parents did not see the need for the process. They wanted the adult child to have rights and independence. So did I, as his teacher. After all, I worked all day, every day to help him be independent. However, we need to be realistic about each developmentally disabled individual's ability to make serious decisions for himself. Each case is different, but if you have a student who can't distinguish between right and wrong or understand why he takes medication or how much a dollar is, then yes, a parent needs to do this. There are no special ed jails and the law does not see their disability in many cases. Even the IEP process does not legally require parents' signatures after 18, or even their presence (if the child did not want them there) without conservatorship papers. I have included in appendix a link explaining the limited conservatorship process.

Transitions for parents of special ed children are not always easy or normal. When parents of regular ed students see their teen graduate from high school, they envision jobs, college, marriage, grandchildren. When parents of SH students see their kids graduate, the parents worry about who will care for them while the parents continue to work to support them. They worry if they can get them a supported job or in a vocational day program which is good. They worry if Medicaid will continue to pay their adult medical expenses. By the way, it is law that private insurance companies cannot drop a disabled adult dependent because of age from parents' policies, although they have to show proof of disability, usually after age 19-25.

Lastly, they worry about what will happen to this child, now an adult, when they die. The parent has finally reached acceptance of their child's disability, probably years before. Now the parent realizes that he is growing older, grayer and more tired. While their child's needs and demands may not have decreased over time, the parents' energy has. Sometimes the child's needs have even increased and finally the parents are forced to face the future and retirement planning with this child for whom they must provide for financially and physically into their golden years and beyond. This means thinking about their own mortality for perhaps the first time. What will happen when they are no longer there to care for him/her? What will happen to their child if the parents die unexpectedly or merely from old age. Many parents of disabled children have said to me, "I hope he goes before I do, because I don't want to think about what will happen to him if I'm not here to care for him." Parents don't usually wish for their children to die before they do. This wish doesn't have to exist if the parent will prepare for their child's independent future. Planning for a group home, a special needs financial trust and conservatorship (to possibly include more than one person to be able to make decisions for him as he ages.)

I will never forget at a home visit of one of my students, a parent told me that when she died her adult son would care for his SH adult sister, her daughter. This young lady, my student, was now 19 and had many behavioral issues. Her brother, who was 22, happened into the room and heard his mother telling me this. He proceeded to tell his 58-year-old, physically handicapped mother, that he wasn't taking care of his sister because he was getting married. It was an awkward moment, but a teachable one, because mom finally realized she needed to make other arrangements for her daughters' future. She had just assumed her other child would be willing without ever discussing it or thinking about the fact that his circumstances might change with his own family.

The role of the educator usually stops at age 22 in public schools, but it is still important for teachers of this age group to understand what the parents face in the future. They grow old with their adult child and although this child, now an adult, has brought them much joy and much heartache, the daily responsibility we all feel as parents never, ever ends for these parents. Parents of SH children never, ever really get to completely let go, even though letting go is, to some extent, necessary and good. Sometimes sadly, letting go means watching a child die, as I had to do. Even in death I learned they have lessons to teach us about how to face death with peace and with courage.

CHAPTER EIGHT

THE FUTURE OF SPECIAL ED

UNTIL 1975 THERE WAS NO SPECIAL EDUCATION FOR ALL children. Now, of course, parents who have a child with a disability can expect that child to get a good education individualized for his abilities and disabilities. Parents have much more hope that their child will achieve some degree of independence and happiness. Individual education plans are developed to plan for an appropriate education regardless of the degree of the child's disability. Transition plans are written to help parents plan for a future for their child after graduation. Job coaches and supported employment means our children are working in the community productively like everyone else in society. Roommate programs, independent living assistance and group homes have replaced institutions so that disabled adults growing old, with or without their even older parents who can no longer provide the physical care and consistency they so need, can live in dignity independently and have a social life. All students are expected to reach standards and have high expectations for their progress.

Change is good. Improvement of programs is continuous. Many special education center schools are closing and more and more students are included in regular education programs. More of society is accepting of people with disabilities as valuable contributing members and no longer see them as objects of pity, curiosity or neglect. They are no longer an invisible minority as they once were hidden away.

Good, dedicated teachers are still, and will always be, needed to help these children become all they can become. You, as a teacher, have chosen this profession because you are needed and you will make a difference. Thirty years from now when you retire from teaching, you will certainly see what a difference these life changing students made in your life and in your relationships and how you perceive the world.

Perhaps that is why these children are born—to make a difference, change lives. Finally, remember that at the end of every teaching day, and especially on Fridays, that you made a difference. You provided a safe haven for your students every day and they left your class more able to do things for themselves and behaving more socially appropriate. Take it one day at a time and remember no matter how slowly the progress is made, it is being made and you are making a difference in their lives. Not everyone is lucky enough to have job where you KNOW every day you make a difference. Both the parents and the children you teach will thank you, even though they may not tell you, you can be sure they are thankful!

APPENDIX

Resources

The National Organization for Rare Disorders (NORD)

https.//www.rarediseases.org

This 501(c)(3) organization, is a unique federation of voluntary health organizations dedicated to helping people with rare "orphan" diseases and assisting the organizations that serve them. NORD is committed to the identification, treatment, and cure of rare disorders through programs of education, advocacy, research, and service.

United Cerebral Palsy

ucp.org

UCP educates, advocates and provides support services to ensure a life without limits for people with a spectrum of disabilities. UCP works to advance the independence, productivity and full citizenship of people with disabilities through an affiliate network that has helped millions.

What Is Down Syndrome? - National Down Syndrome Society

www.ndss.org

Research and support organization for families with Down syndrome.

Seizure Tracker®

https://www.seizuretracker.com/

Free seizure tracker tools and printable logs to record seizure activity. Free online tools to provide people living with epilepsy and their doctors with a better understanding of the relationship between seizures and a student's functioning.

Autism Organizations - Autism Speaks

www.autismspeaks.org

> Association for Science in Autism Treatment (ASAT) Not-for-profit organization of parents and professionals committed to improving the education, treatment.

The National Autism Association | Serving the most urgent needs of the Autism Community.

www.autism-society.org/

> Causes of Autism - Big Red Safety Box | FOUND - Autism Fact Sheet - Helping Hand professionals committed to improving the education, treatment.

Epilepsy Foundation

www.epilepsy.com/

> Information, community and resources about epilepsy. Types of Seizures - An Introduction to Epilepsy - Chat - About Epilepsy & Seizures.

What Is TSC? - Tuberous Sclerosis Alliance

TSalliance.org

> Tuberous sclerosis complex (TSC) is a genetic disorder that causes non- malignant tumors to form in many different organs, primarily in the brain, eye, kidney. TSC is a research and family support organization.

Parenting Special Needs Magazine

parentingspecialneeds.org/

> Help parents navigate the uncharted waters of raising a special needs child. Providing practical tips, sharing life's lessons, tackling the challenges.

Dads 4 Special Kids (D4SK)

dads4specialkids.org/

> We discuss issues that impact our members, host topics that

encourage maturity in the role of being a dad in the journey of raising a child with special needs

The 15 Best Websites for Parents of Special Needs Children ...

www.special-education-degree.net/the-best-websites-for- parents-of-special needs children…

Raising a child with special needs can be difficult enough, but thanks to the worldwide web, the Internet is full of tons of informational websites … this site lists many good ones to share with your parents.

Tips for Happier, More Productive IEP Meetings | TeachHUB

www.teachhub.com/iep-meeting-tips

An IEP meeting (or any parent-teacher meeting) may turn tense in a hurry if a parent: ... more before the meeting with some good news, you are showing the parent that ... By taking a minute at the end of the meeting to ask if they understand .

ep Magazine or Exceptional Parent

www.eparent.com/

Magazine for parents of children or young adults with disabilities. Includes reports, forum, products links, books.

What is a Limited Conservatorship - California Courts

www.courts.ca.gov/partners/documents/

A limited conservatorship of the person is a court arrangement where a conservator cares for and protects a developmentally disabled adult and provides legal oversight self help packet for the limited conservatorship of the person www.sdcourt.ca.gov/pls/portal/docs/PAGE/.../PKT030.PDF

This information is a good resource but conservatorship requirements vary from state to state. Regional center worker will also have handouts for you to give parents if you ask.

Sample Forms

Many SE students are non verbal or have limited speech so the more you know about home life the better you can reach this student to teach him or her- you can add more or different questions - make sure they are culturally and socially sensitive questions which will help you understand the child.

Questionnaire and questions to ask or send home for parents to fill out before interview or IEP. Send two copies home

Student name ⎯⎯⎯⎯⎯⎯⎯⎯⎯⎯⎯⎯⎯⎯⎯⎯⎯⎯⎯⎯

Birth date ⎯⎯⎯⎯⎯⎯⎯⎯⎯⎯⎯⎯⎯⎯⎯⎯⎯⎯⎯⎯⎯⎯

Teacher room no. ⎯⎯⎯⎯⎯⎯⎯⎯⎯⎯⎯⎯⎯⎯⎯⎯⎯⎯

School phone ⎯⎯⎯⎯⎯⎯⎯⎯⎯⎯⎯⎯⎯⎯⎯⎯⎯⎯⎯⎯

Please return this to your child's teacher before IEP meeting and bring your copy to the IEP meeting.

What language does your child hear at home or use the most? ⎯⎯

⎯⎯⎯⎯⎯⎯⎯⎯⎯⎯⎯⎯⎯⎯⎯⎯⎯⎯⎯⎯⎯⎯⎯⎯⎯⎯⎯⎯⎯

What are your child's strengths? ⎯⎯⎯⎯⎯⎯⎯⎯⎯⎯⎯⎯⎯⎯

What suggestions do you have of ways to help your child learn? ⎯⎯

⎯⎯⎯⎯⎯⎯⎯⎯⎯⎯⎯⎯⎯⎯⎯⎯⎯⎯⎯⎯⎯⎯⎯⎯⎯⎯⎯⎯⎯

What are your most important goals for your child this year? ⎯⎯⎯

⎯⎯⎯⎯⎯⎯⎯⎯⎯⎯⎯⎯⎯⎯⎯⎯⎯⎯⎯⎯⎯⎯⎯⎯⎯⎯⎯⎯⎯

What is happening at school that you would like to see continue and see as important? ⎯⎯⎯⎯⎯⎯⎯⎯⎯⎯⎯⎯⎯⎯⎯⎯⎯⎯⎯⎯⎯

What activities does your child enjoy most at home and at school? ⎯⎯

⎯⎯⎯⎯⎯⎯⎯⎯⎯⎯⎯⎯⎯⎯⎯⎯⎯⎯⎯⎯⎯⎯⎯⎯⎯⎯⎯⎯⎯

Who does your child spend most of his time with? Who does he live with and what are their names and relationships? ⎯⎯⎯⎯⎯⎯⎯⎯⎯

⎯⎯⎯⎯⎯⎯⎯⎯⎯⎯⎯⎯⎯⎯⎯⎯⎯⎯⎯⎯⎯⎯⎯⎯⎯⎯⎯⎯⎯

What methods do you use or think will help motivate your child?

_____

Any other thing you want to include or have questions about before
the IEP meeting which will help us help your child?? _____

Thank you for completing this!! _____

Person completing this form _____

Date _____

Positive motivators questionnaire

What does the child like to eat the most? drink? snacks, healthy foods?
sweets? regular meals? etc. _____

What does he/she not like? _____

What does he/she like to do at home? tv shows? computer? play out
doors? exercise? prepare snacks? help with chores? visit familyfriends?

_____

What does he like to do on play ground (if appropriate) team games?
play alone? play equipment? _____

What does he like to do in the classroom? hands on activities? com
puter? art? time with teacher? group activities? specific subjects? ____
therapy time? _____

_____

What does he like to do in the community? shopping? church? visit
family? friends? Sports? library?

_____

Social reinforcers? school and home? to reward him for good behavior
or good effort?? _____

Does your child like public praise? private praise? high five? rewards?
stickers? computer time? time with parent? special trip to movie, ____
library, playground?? special treat? time with special friend?? Hobby
time? _____

Information teacher needs to know as SOON AS possible!

Your school should provide these forms for you or design your own.

You need to know :

- Child's name, nickname and age
- Diagnosis, if there is one
- Who is parent or guardian and ALWAYS have a emergency contact!!! Never release child to anyone not designated!
- Where he goes to get medical attention and who is his primary doctor? dentist?
- Does he wear glasses, hearing aid? require any special assistance?
- Medication being taken - why and what and dosage - your school nurse and emergency forms will require this but make sure you always have copy with you .
- Seizure activity if any and duration of seizures
- Toileting routine
- Eating or sleeping problems
- Any particular behavior or phobia or fear you need to be aware of
- ANY FOOD or other allergies — and make sure you are aware and remember on field trips etc
- The things he likes the most and the things he hates the most especially if he is non-verbal.
- Who are the important people and pets in his life - names and ages and who he lives with and who is his caretaker/ sitter if he has one.

Sample Letters

- Some sample positive class-wide note - send quarterly or weekly.
- Remember these kids can't answer "How was school today?"
- Some teachers send a daily schedule/pictogram home so parents have talking points and know what their child did daily.

Good News!
_____ learned how to _____today!
Give him a hug!
We are all so proud of this accomplishment!
Mr./Ms._____ (teacher name)

Good News!
_____ finished his IEP goal of_____

_____
He did an outstanding job!
Mr./Ms. _____

Good News!
_____ had excellent behavior today! Big improvement!
Congratulations!
Mr./Ms. _____

Good News!
_____ finished all his work today!
He did a great job staying focused!
Mr./Ms. _____

Dear parents,

The class in room _____ is making great progress on their IEP goals and learning many new things this year.

Thank you so much for your support and for promptly returning the many forms and questions I sent home. It helps me so much to understand your child's needs!

I really appreciate each of you making time to check your child's backpack daily for notes and messages and for letting me know of any changes in health, medication or sleep patterns or problems.

Thank you for sharing your child with me this year! Each student is such a joy to teach and adds so much to my life.!

If you have any concerns during the year you can please call me at _____ after ___pm when students are not in the room, or send me a note and I will get back to you.

Thank you again and happy Friday!!

Mr./Ms._____

What is a Limited Conservatorship?

There are several types of conservatorships. One special type of conservatorship is called the **limited conservatorship.** This is when a judge appoints a responsible person (called a **conservator**) to assist an adult with developmental disabilities (called a **conservatee**) who is unable to provide for her/his personal and/or financial needs.

There are 2 kinds of limited conservatorships:

A **limited conservatorship of the person** is a court arrangement where a conservator cares for and protects a developmentally disabled adult and provides for the conservatee's needs associated with daily life.

A **limited conservatorship of the estate** is a court arrangement where a conservator handles the conservatee's financial matters - like paying bills and collecting the conservatee's income if the conservatee has an estate.

How will I know if I also need to be a limited conservator of the estate?

You *do not* need a conservatorship of the estate if:

- the developmentally disabled adult you care for gets public assistance, like Supplemental Security Income (SSI) or Social Security (SSA) but has no other assets, or
- If the developmentally disabled adult earns a wage.

But, you *need* a conservatorship of the estate if the developmentally disabled adult has other assets, such as an inheritance or a settlement from a lawsuit that is not in a special needs trust.

Note: This manual addresses conservatorship of the person only.

When is a bond required?

A bond is required in most conservatorship of the estate to guarantee proper performance of the duties of the conservator of the estate. If you are appointed only as conservator of the person you need not file a bond unless required by the court.

Who decides if the adult is developmentally disabled?

An adult with developmental disabilities is someone who has severe and chronic disabilities because of a mental or physical impairment.

The **Regional Center** in your community will test the proposed conservatee to see if she/he is develop- mentally disabled. If the Regional Center accepted the person as a consumer (or client) before age eighteen (18), then she/he automatically qualifies as a person with developmental disabilities. But, if the person has never been tested or accepted as a regional center consumer, she/he must be tested.

If the Regional Center feels that individual does not qualify as a person with developmental disabilities, and you disagree, you can appeal to the Area Board in your region (created by the state legislature to advocate for the rights of individuals with developmental disabilities.

When should I apply for limited conservatorship?

If you are trying to establish a limited conservator- ship for someone who will soon be 18 years old, it's a good idea to start the process more than 3 months before the developmentally disabled person's 18th birthday. However, you can establish a limited conservatorship at any time after the person with the developmental disability has reached age 18.

Who can be appointed as limited conservator?

Any adult can file for conservatorship. Conservators are usually parents, sisters, or brothers, but any responsible adult can act as conservator. And, there can be more than one limited conservator.

What All Limited Conservators Need To Know!

What kind of decisions can a limited conservator make?

A limited conservator's duty is to help the limited conservatee *develop maximum self-reliance and independence.* Because developmentally disabled adults can usually do many things on their own, the judge will only give the limited conservator power to do things the conservatee cannot do without help.

After the hearing the limited conservator's *"Letters of Conservatorship"* and the *"Order Appointing Probate Conservator"* will list the exact areas (powers) in which the limited conservator is authorized to act.

What powers can a limited conservator ask for?

A limited conservator may ask the court to give you the following 7 powers:

- Fix the conservatee's residence or dwelling
- Access the conservatee's confidential records or paper
- Consent or withhold consent to marriage on behalf of the conservatee
- Enter into contracts on behalf of the conservatee
- Give or withhold medical consent on behalf of the conservatee
- Select the conservatee's social and sexual contacts and relationships
- Make decisions to educate the conservatee

What are the Responsibilities of a Limited Conservator?

As a limited conservator of the person, you must take care of the conservatee's:

- Food,
- Clothing,
- Shelter, and
- Well-being.

For more information refer to the *Handbook for Conservators*, published by the Judicial Council of California and available at the Probate Clerk's window for a fee. The handbook is also available on the internet: http://www.courtinfo.ca.gov/selfhelp/seniors/ handbook.htm

Made in the USA
San Bernardino, CA
27 July 2016